Families

Family Homes

Debbie Gallagher

Marshall Cavendish
Benchmark
New York

This edition first published in 2009 in the United States of America by Marshall Cavendish Benchmark.

Marshall Cavendish Benchmark
99 White Plains Road
Tarrytown, NY 10591
www.marshallcavendish.us

All Internet sites were available and accurate when sent to press.

First published in 2008 by
MACMILLAN EDUCATION AUSTRALIA PTY LTD
15–19 Claremont St, South Yarra 3141

Visit our Web site at www.macmillan.com.au or go directly to www.macmillanlibrary.com.au

Associated companies and representatives throughout the world.

Library of Congress Cataloging-in-Publication Data

Gallagher, Debbie, 1969-
    Family homes / by Debbie Gallagher.
        p. cm. — (Families)
    Includes index.
    ISBN 978-0-7614-3136-7
    1. Dwellings—Juvenile literature. 2. Family—Juvenile literature. I. Title.
    TH4811.5.G353 2008
392.3'6—dc22
                                            2008001667

Edited by Georgina Garner
Text and cover design by Christine Deering
Page layout by Raul Diche
Photo research by Brendan Gallagher

Printed in the United States

Acknowledgments
The author and the publisher are grateful to the following for permission to reproduce copyright material:

Front cover photograph: Family outside their home © Getty Images/Photodisc

Photos courtesy of: © Chris Jewiss/123RF, **5**; Corbis Royalty Free, **3**, **23**; Duncraig Castle, **13**; Flat Earth, **10**; © Getty Images/AsiaPix, **19**; © Getty Images/Collection Mix, **27**; © Getty Images/Digital Vision, **21**; © Getty Images/Photodisc, **1**; © andres balcazar/iStockphoto, **25**; © Glenn Frank/iStockphoto, **8**; © Alexander Hafemann/iStockphoto, **16**; © slobo mitic/iStockphoto, **14**; © Pavel Pospisil/iStockphoto, **12**; © Chris Ronneseth/iStockphoto, **11**; © Daniela Andreea Spyropoulos/iStockphoto, **18**; © Nick Stubbs/iStockphoto, **15**; © Alan Tobey/iStockphoto, **17**; © Peeter Viisimaa/iStockphoto, **22**; Photodisc, **4**; Photo-Easy.com, **9**; Photos.com, **6**, **7**, **28**; SassyStock Royalty Free, **26**; Bill Lyons/*Saudi Aramco World*/PADIA, **24**; © Jaimie Duplass/Shutterstock, **20**; © Jeanne Hatch/Shutterstock, **29**.

While every care has been taken to trace and acknowledge copyright, the publisher tenders their apologies for any accidental infringement where copyright has proved untraceable. Where the attempt has been unsuccessful, the publisher welcomes information that would redress the situation.

1 3 5 6 4 2

Contents

Glossary words

When a word is printed in **bold**, you can look up its meaning in the Glossary on page 31.

Families

Families live in countries all around the world. Some of your friends may have a family just like yours. Some of your friends may have families very different from yours.

Families are made up of people of different ages.

A family home is where a family lives. Homes are often houses or **apartments**, but some families live in tents, boats, and caves.

Some families in Cambodia live in homes built over water.

Family Homes

In most homes, there are people belonging to one family or more. Sometimes, there are parents and children. Sometimes, the family includes grandparents, uncles, aunts, and cousins.

A family builds a home together.

A family home is a place where families can care for one another. They share meals, stories, and games together. A home is also where people relax and sleep.

Two brothers read together in their home.

Different Types of Homes

Like families, homes come in different shapes and sizes. Many homes are houses that are divided into separate rooms. These different rooms are used for different purposes, such as cooking.

This Japanese house has thin walls that divide it into rooms.

In many hot African countries, separate grass or mud huts make up a home. Often, a fence will group these huts together.

Each hut is used for a different purpose, such as sleeping or storing food.

Mobile Homes

Some family homes are **mobile**. These homes can move with the family if the family decides to move to another place. Boats are a type of mobile home.

Sampan boats are home to families who live in Hong Kong's harbor.

Nomadic people have homes that are mobile. These homes are often tents, or mobile homes that are pulled by horses or cars.

Nomadic families in Mongolia live in *ger* tents, which they pack up and move.

Unusual Homes

Some homes are unusual. Some are built on stilts over water. This allows families to get to fishing areas quickly and easily.

Families that live in houses over water use boats to reach their homes.

In Europe, some families live in old castles. The families that first lived in these castles were **royalty** or **nobility.**

Some castles are still home to noble families.

Shelter and Protection

A home provides a family with shelter and protection from the weather. A family can escape rain, wind, snow, heat, and cold inside their home.

The roof of a house stops the rain from getting everything wet.

Most homes can be heated when it is cold outside. When it is hot, curtains are closed to keep the sunlight out.

Windows are sometimes opened to let in a cool breeze.

Protection from Heat

In the Sahara Desert, some families build homes under the ground. These homes stay cool, even when it is hot above the ground. The families are protected from the heat.

Houses built under the ground stay cool.

Protection from Sandstorms

In northern Africa, the Tuareg people live in tents. If there is a sandstorm, the family closes the sides of the tent. This keeps the sand out.

The sides of the tent are removed to let in cool breezes.

Sharing Time and Space

Family members share time and space together in a home. The home is a place where family members feel they belong.

A mother and daughter share time together doing the dishes.

Some family members spend most of the day away from home. Older family members might go out to work while younger family members go to school.

A family spend their evening together doing a jigsaw puzzle.

Feeling Safe and Cared For

Homes are not just places for relaxing, sleeping, and eating. A home is a place where everyone in a family can feel safe and loved.

A home is a place where family members watch over one another.

When a family member is sick, other members may take care of that person at home.

A father looks after his sick son at home.

Private Spaces

Family members can have their own **private** space in a home. In some homes, the most private space is the bedroom.

This boy's private space is an area of the house away from people.

Having a private space in the home gives people a place to express themselves. Some people like to decorate their private space.

Children can keep toys and pictures in and around their private space.

Work Spaces

Part of a home can also be a work space. Some people work in the home instead of going away from home to work.

Painting pottery is a job that can be done at home.

In some homes, there is a separate space for an office, workshop, **studio**, or study. People do their work there and then deliver or send it where it is needed.

Home offices may have equipment such as telephones and computers.

Learning Spaces

Homes can be places for family members to learn new **skills** or interests. Older members might teach younger ones something new.

A mother helps her son with his school studies.

Some families like to learn how to make music together. They might do this in a music room. Large homes sometimes have a library, where books can be read, or an art studio.

Art can be done in a home studio.

Family Activities

Families often share favorite activities in and around the home. Some families play games, such as cards and chess. Some families like growing flowers and vegetables in their gardens.

A mother teaches her daughter how to water the flowers.

Some homes have space for a pet inside the house or in a yard. In an apartment, a family might keep a pet bird or fish.

Children who live on farms may have large pets, such as horses.

A Floor Plan

A floor plan is a drawing showing the layout of an area in a home or room. It is drawn as a bird's-eye view, seen from above.

Try this!

Draw a floor plan of your bedroom.

Anna's Room

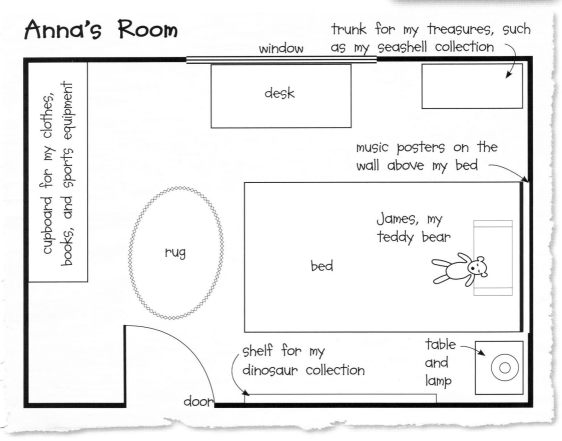

window

trunk for my treasures, such as my seashell collection

desk

cupboard for my clothes, books, and sports equipment

music posters on the wall above my bed

rug

James, my teddy bear

bed

shelf for my dinosaur collection

table and lamp

door

30

Glossary

apartments   separate homes in one building

mobile   able to move

nobility   the ruling class in a community

nomadic people   people who do not live in one particular place but who move about

private   something that is yours and not shared with other people

royalty   kings, queens, and their families

skills   things you can do well

studio   a room in which an artist works

Index